I have learned that believing in very different things. For so ma can find ourselves coasting—d without ever moving out of first gear. Often it's not until life throws us a curveball that we are forced to really stop and think deeply about our relationship with God and what it actually means in practice.

Getting a cancer diagnosis is one of the scariest things that a person can go through. And for Kerrie Ann, having the memory of her own mother's battle with cancer must have added an even more tangible reality to an already terrifying situation. Reading her words as she describes each step of her journey, from her first suspicions to the investigations, being given the diagnosis, and each step of the treatment, we can truly feel just how real it was.

What I find most inspiring about following her journey through her battle with cancer is how she never once pretended it was simple. She didn't put on a fake smile or try to show how being Christian made the journey easy. She tells it as it is and allows us to feel everything she felt.

But we also get to experience the unmistakable power of God at work in her life. We get to see what happened when she allowed God to take absolute control. We get to see the limitless power of faith— how every time the battle tried to push her to the edge, her faith made her stronger and kept her focused on the prize! She shows us that when we allow God to be glorified even in the midst of our challenges, he can make the impossible possible. We see how even the greatest battle can be fought with grace, courage, and, most of all, joy.

No matter where you are in your walk with God, this book is for you. Whether you've experienced your own major battles and made it out the other side, you're currently in the midst of one, or yours are yet to come, I encourage you to let Kerrie Ann's story inspire and challenge you to see for yourself what happens when you allow God to take His rightful place at the centre of our lives at all times, even and especially in our darkest hours.

**Dr. Adjoa M. Kyei-Sarpong**

Kerrie Ann's book is an outstanding piece! In this work, a timeless resource is revealed to inspire the broken-hearted, a handbook for those with challenging health conditions, all lovers of triumph, and a discourse that honestly reflects victory in adversity and the beauty of good relationships.

This book unveils a moving and inspiring true-life story of a winner —a woman of valour with eyes of faith, with the heart of a champion, and with unspeakable gratitude and passion to uplift others through what she suffered.

I am amazed by the revelations from this beautiful heart who, by divine grace, overcame through faith, by the blood of the Lamb, and by the words of her testimonies.

It all began out of the blue with a lump that shockingly ended up in a biopsy report as the dreaded "C word"—a difficult journey!

The trigger to her contacting her doctor in a telling manner is not without a love story that underlines the beauty of couples working together in unity, as captured in Ecclesiastes 4:9-12.

Diagnosed with breast cancer in the prime of her life despite her healthy lifestyle, it seemed as if she had lost everything. But she would not bow to fear or gloom, and instead of letting the unhelpful circumstances of her diagnosis define her, she found hope in misery, wore garments of faith, became purpose-driven, and redefined her life with fortitude, vision, and new priorities.

Despite the harrowing experiences of her treatments, her strength was divinely made perfect in weakness. She persevered in faith and thrived in her conviction that although weeping may endure for a night, joy cometh in the morning.

Chapter by chapter, you will read the inspiring account of this incredible woman's journey, the pains, difficulties, and resilience, the support of friends, her children and caring husband, her mother, the prayers, and the God-inspired hope that won the battle.

You will benefit from the distilled wisdom in this book, and may you be blessed as you read.

I commend it to you.

**Dr. Ikechukwu Joshua Madumere**
Medical Practitioner, Whitstable, Kent.
Author and Minister of The Gospel, Redeemed Christian Church of God.

It is a great honour to be able to comment on this story. As the title of one of Pastor John Ameobi's books go, we are to *"Give God Something to Work With."* Thus, Kerrie Ann has given her story, her journey of battling breast cancer, to God so that He may work with it to bring encouragement to many.

The book highlights her low points and where she gets her strength. I strongly recommend it to all as a guide to seek blessings no matter the battle.

**Dr. Olugbenga Ayodele Afolabi**
Respiratory Consultant

I believe your book will be a true blessing to people, not only in a similar situation to what you had but also to those facing deliberating illnesses or chronic illnesses. It is full of encouragement and showcases rising above very challenging situations. It demonstrates your strong faith and complete dependence on God. Undoubtedly, it will encourage people of no faith and help strengthen those who have faith. Well done for writing a book during a tough time in your life.

**Sarah**
Kerrie's neighbour who works for the NHS

# WINGS OF COURAGE

# WINGS OF COURAGE

## BLOSSOMING WITH HOPE IN THE FACE OF CANCER

KERRIE ANN **HARRISON**

**ISBN:** 9798853740365

**Bible versions used include:**
English Standard Version **(ESV)**. ESV® Text Edition: 2016.
Copyright © 2001 by Crossway Bibles, a publishing ministry of
Good News Publishers; **The Message (MSG)** Copyright © 1993,
2002, 2018 by Eugene H. Peterson; New International Version
**(NIV)** Holy Bible, New International Version®, NIV® Copyright
©1973, 1978, 1984, 2011 by Biblica, Inc.® Used by permission. All
rights reserved worldwide; **New Living Translation (NLT)** *Holy
Bible*, New Living Translation, copyright © 1996, 2004, 2015 by
Tyndale House Foundation. Used by permission of Tyndale House
Publishers, Inc., Carol Stream, Illinois 60188. All rights reserved.;
The Passion Translation **(TPT)** The Passion Translation®.
Copyright © 2017 by BroadStreet Publishing® Group, LLC. Used
by permission. All rights reserved. thePassionTranslation.com

Publisher Details
**WordAlive**
hello@josephkolawole.org
www.josephkolawole.org
+447752398481

# Contents

*To my children: Lakemfa, Timiebi, Tahlia, and Elicia Harrison. When I was in the darkest period of my life, it was love for you that kept me going. Thank you for standing strong, teaching me to laugh and have fun in the middle of the storm. Love you all very much.*

*In memory of my parents, Mr & Mrs M & A Lynch, for all the love, help, and support you showed me and the sacrifices you made. I know that you are both watching over me. Mum, you taught me the definition of courage and overcoming fear. Dad, you showed me how to live with confidence as you lived life with infectious energy.*

*This book is dedicated to all those special people who supported me during this difficult journey.*

*The book is also dedicated to my loving heavenly Father God for the grace to get this book published.*

# Introduction

This book is about a period in my life when I was diagnosed with the news that everyone dreads: cancer. In this book, I talk about my diagnosis, treatment, the challenges that came with cancer, and how I stood up to this dreaded disease while finding hope in the face of adversity. I do hope that readers will find it inspiring and moving in some way. Cancer was a catalyst in my life, as I decided that no matter what it would take, I would be happy and make gratitude a part of my life to help me navigate through this difficult time. Cancer gave me a different perspective through which to see the world, and for that, I am grateful. It was a blessing to have gone through this experience because it revealed the clarity of life and death. This experience helped me gain wings for a better and brighter future while holding onto the life raft of hope. This book is dedicated to all those who are undergoing cancer, their families, and friends, so that they may be encouraged and supported to create a new beginning. *Wings of Courage* is also dedicated to all those people who helped me during this traumatic time in my life and played a role in my journey. I am grateful to God for His strength, love, and grace that sustained me and brought me through triumphantly. This period in my life taught me the things that truly matter, such as joy, gratitude, connections, purpose, vitality, and possibilities.

My belief is that I am a traveller on this journey of life on earth, much like being on a plane travelling through the days and years to various destinations, and the decisions we make along the way impact the journey. On board this plane are many passengers—friends, family, those who touch our lives, and those whom we impact. The things I have learned along the way all contribute to the journey, making it powerful. This is why it is important not to look back and to be content in the present moment, as we are heading towards a great destination. As a young girl, I decided that I would do my best on this journey and fully immerse myself in it. I was also going to do my best as I embarked on this challenging journey. The challenge was to remain focused and positive, to put into perspective that it's not all about the destination, and to embrace enjoying my life in the present. I survived because God had a reason to keep me alive, and that reason is worth the battle.

I was enjoying life in my early forties, busy with four young children, working as a key worker in the midst of lockdown, trying to lose weight - like many others - busy with cross-country running, and did not anticipate adding breast cancer to my list of challenges. The dreaded cancer came at the wrong time in my life when I had so much to do and achieve, and I was living life to the fullest. Let's be honest, it was really beginning to get on my nerves, as it would take away so much time from my life and precious family. We had so much to do, and then this shocking news arrived unexpectedly. For goodness sake, I was still relatively young at the age of 43. However, I did not wait for my circumstances to improve; rather, I used this period to improve myself. I dared to believe that the days ahead would be greater and better than this dark season. This diagnosis proved to be pivotal in my life, and I am grateful that I was able to use it to reset my priorities and outlook on life. I was determined to create a life that was unbreakable and full of joy.

When faced with the unexpected and devastating news of cancer, I had to cling to my source of hope for strength in the midst of the storm. I had to live with true bravery. How this battle is won depends on you. How does one prepare?

As painful as it is, you can still thrive and make it work for you. The keynote of my cancer journey is *"remaining hopeful on the journey, soaring upon eagle's wings"* (hence, the book title, *Wings of Courage*). This speaks of rising and soaring—like an eagle—above the storm of cancer and not letting it limit my life in any way. I was not going to allow cancer to constantly define my life, as I knew that it was a temporary season that would not last forever. Eagles are majestic creatures and they are not weighed down by circumstances; rather, they are champions of the sky. This demanding journey has been used to shape my life and to overcome fears that at times hold us back from reaching greater heights. In this book, I talk about finding the positives in a traumatic experience and how to move forward. Love, connections, and my spiritual life matter to me. I could not have made it through without the special people around me who were so loving and kind, and who were praying for me to keep me afloat. It is incredibly difficult to feel self-pity when there are so many people caring, reaching out, praying, and thinking of you. Also, the prayers from my close friends during those moments when I was extremely ill provided me with the fortitude to continue pressing on. There is no way that I can ever express my appreciation to them fully, but it is profound and enduring.

- **Important moment 1:** It was May 2020 during lockdown. I was playing around with the children at home, doing Joe Wicks' fitness programme - a push-up, to be precise - when I felt a very slight pain on my left side from my armpit towards my breast. I thought it was simply because I needed to improve my upper body strength and did not think much more about it.

- **Important moment 2:** This came two weeks later when I woke up from deep sleep with intense pain in my left breast. I knew then that it was time to call the GP and get this checked out. However, as we were in the middle of lockdown, it proved difficult and required a telephone triage at first. I persisted and eventually got an appointment. The GP could not feel anything at all upon examination, but to be on the safe side, I was referred to the hospital for a mammogram.

- **Important moment 3:** This happened two days later. My left breast was sore and painful. I then felt a lump, and I knew something was wrong. This was the moment at which the journey began.

There is nothing pleasant about cancer. Nothing prepares you for it; it comes like a plague without warning, and so the journey begins. I was about to embark on the most painful journey of my life. Unless one has been through this journey themselves, they may not be able to comprehend how difficult it is, but there is hope and power in the process. You may not understand why, but there is a purpose to this journey. Your life is not over. I was determined not to wallow in self-pity and feel sorry for myself. Having lost my mother to cancer, I was determined that cancer was not going to deprive me of my abundant life. My mother always taught me that your thoughts eventually become your actions. So, to be content and happy, it comes down to one's outlook on life. Many times I was in tears from pain and exhaustion, but one thing I did was give my absolute best so that the outcome would be good. At first, I was angry about this period of inactivity in my life while undergoing cancer treatment. But then I had to console myself, surrender, refocus, readjust, and keep going. I was going to do what needed to be done. I was determined that in this journey, I was not going to fail, but to come out victorious. That was my mindset. Cancer served a purpose in my life. I saw cancer as a gift because I am now living my best life. Out of this affliction and anguish came a new perspective and a greater love for life. I underwent a complete transformation regarding my health and mindset. If I had not gone through this cancer journey, I would never have had the courage, strength, and resilience I have today. I have emerged as a different person. To reiterate, I did not do it alone; the overwhelming kindness and support I received from friends, family, church, and strangers was truly overwhelming. This made all the difference, as so many people were fighting this battle with me and provided encouragement. So many people were counting on me, and I needed to keep going. I would not bow down to fear when cancer struck because I soon realised I was stronger than I thought.

As you read this, forgive the back and forth in my tenses. This is because some of the chapters were written as journal entries during the journey while some were written as I reflect on the experience in retrospect. In any case, I am glad to echo the praise of Apostle Paul,

*All praise to the God and Father of our Master, Jesus the Messiah! Father of all mercy! God of all healing counsel! He comes alongside us when we go through hard times, and before you know it, he brings us alongside someone else who is going through hard times so that we can be there for that person just as God was there for us.*

— 2 CORINTHIANS 1:3-4 MSG

He is the God of all healing counsel who came alongside me with comfort and help when I went through my cancer journey. It is my joy to pay it forward.

Happy Reading!

# CHAPTER 1

# The Beginning of It All

"The problem is not to find the answer; it's to face the answer."

— TERENCE MCKENNA

## MAY 2020

It is May 2020, in the midst of the lockdown. Thanks to the coronavirus, my life is filled with numerous responsibilities. Being a mother of four young children, my days are incredibly hectic. I constantly juggle my roles as a mother, housekeeper, professional, fitness enthusiast, and churchgoer, leaving very little time for myself. I rely on God's strength each day as I wake up, determined to maintain my energy levels.

I have always been passionate about fitness since my youth. I have never smoked, and alcohol has never touched my lips. I breastfed all four of my children, follow a healthy diet, and possess a positive outlook on life. There were no signs or symptoms in my body indicating that I had cancer. I enjoyed excellent health and exercised daily. I underwent all routine examinations and had an abundance of energy. However, there is a family history of breast cancer on my mother's side.

Finally, the weekend arrives. I am playing with my children at home, engaging in Joe Wicks' fitness program. During a push-up, I feel a very slight pain on my left side, extending from my armpit towards my breast. I assume it's due to the need for improvement in my upper body strength and don't dwell on it further. Life continues as usual. Little do I know, my life is about to take an unexpected turn.

Important moment 2 occurs two weeks later when I am abruptly awakened from a deep sleep by intense pain in my left breast. I realise it is time to call the GP and have it checked. However, in the midst of the lockdown, getting an appointment proves to be challenging, resulting in a telephone triage initially. I persist and eventually secure an appointment on June 9th, 2020, at 12 noon. During the GP's examination, there is no indication of anything abnormal. No lump or sign of concern. However, to err on the side of caution, I am referred to the hospital for a mammogram. My mind is filled with various unpleasant thoughts, but I reassure myself that since no lump can be felt, it may be just a cyst. I am given an appointment at the Breast Clinic for Thursday, June 25th, at 3.30 pm.

Important moment 3 occurs on June 20th, approximately a week after my GP appointment. My left breast becomes sore and painful. It is then that I feel a lump. There are still five days remaining until my scheduled mammogram. I sense that something is wrong. Could it be life-threatening? I have to wait until my appointment at the hospital to find out. The battle begins within my mind and emotions as I contemplate the potential diagnosis. As a Christian, I turn to God, seeking His peace and strength in the midst of this situation, and then carry on with my daily routine. My friends and family reassure me that there is nothing to worry about, that it is likely just a cyst.

# CHAPTER 2

## The Dreaded 'C' Word

"You have to accept whatever comes and the only important thing is that you meet it with courage and with the best that you have to give."

— ELEANOR ROOSEVELT

Finally, the day arrives for my visit to the Breast Clinic at the hospital. Due to the coronavirus and the lockdown restrictions, I am not allowed to have anyone accompany me for moral support. Therefore, I must summon extra bravery and face the appointment alone. The morning readings have taught me valuable lessons. Isaiah 52 mentions the phrase "put on," which reminds me to embrace strength and courage. It may not align with my natural disposition or how I am feeling, but I choose to put on God's strength.

The clinic is bustling with activity. I am instructed to remove my top and bra and don a hospital gown. Calmly, I take a seat in the waiting area, anticipating my name to be called. Soon, a nurse guides me into a room for my mammogram, which proves to be uncomfortable. It involves standing against a large machine with a metal plate that pulls, compresses, and squeezes each breast. Following that, I proceed to the scan room for an ultrasound. A male radiographer sits at a computer adjacent to the couch where I lie, while a nurse provides reassurance and uses a lubricated wand to examine my breast. Then comes the shock. The radiographer informs me that there is a suspicious lump and a biopsy is necessary to determine if it is cancerous. The nurse offers sympathy and engages in conversation. Needles are my absolute dread, and I nearly faint with shock when they produce a large needle. I won't hide the fact that it was excruciatingly painful. Under local anaesthesia, they extract not just one, but four tissue samples from my left breast. In a daze, I am comforted by the nurse, who informs me that I will likely experience significant bruising the next day.

After further waiting, I am called to see the breast consultant. The sombre expression on my consultant's face confirms that something is amiss. The mammogram and ultrasound scan have revealed a suspicious lump that may indicate cancer in my breast. I am instructed to return in a week's time to receive the biopsy results. Speechless and shocked, I must summon courage and strength to carry on as usual, particularly for the sake of my children. Numerous people are counting on me. I wish I could have taken Shadrach, my partner, with me, as his presence not only provides support but also helps in remembering everything the consultant shares during such a state of shock.

Life must continue as normal after the biopsy, with the usual routine of caring for my children, managing their schooling, work, homework, activities, and church commitments. The weather is pleasant over the weekend, so we take the children for a walk, enjoying the sunshine and indulging in fish and chips. There is something truly delightful about being outdoors, especially when the sun is shining. I revel in nature's beauty and tranquillity, finding solace and renewal for my soul. My follow-up appointment for the biopsy results is scheduled for Thursday, July 2nd, 2020.

Until the biopsy results are revealed, I remain uncertain whether the lump is benign or malignant. I can't believe this is happening. Nonetheless, I continue to wear a brave face and carry on as usual. As a Christian, I believe that God is in control and will provide me with His grace to navigate through this ordeal. However, it is still an anxious time, and I continually remind myself that I am not alone, for God and my family are by my side.

A multitude of thoughts swirl through my mind as dark clouds loom above me. I can choose to focus on the negatives or dwell on the positives, recalling promises and affirming words that strengthen me. So, I take heart and proclaim aloud, "God is with me, and everything is working together for my good." I trust that I will eventually witness the occurrence of small miracles in my life.

I have made the firm decision not merely to endure this journey, but to fight and emerge from this situation as a conqueror. Initially, upon receiving the diagnosis, I said to my children, "No, God took my mother at an early age, and I don't want to go through this again." I will fight for the sake of my children.

After much reflection, I surrender myself to God, acknowledging that my life is in His hands.

Furthermore, my mother's story is not my own; we each have unique paths. I yearn for peace and reassurance. Turning to the Bible and offering prayers to God, I find comfort and resilience in various passages. Psalm 91 resonates deeply: "You are hidden in the strength of God Most High. He's the hope that holds me and the stronghold to shelter me, my great confidence." These words provide a calm amidst the storm. I rest in His love for me, knowing that this is but a temporary season I will traverse, and it will not endure. This realisation affirms that there is purpose in this journey and that those around me will be impacted. My family prays alongside me, offering encouragement and strengthening my faith that this situation will ultimately end well. I begin to embrace the belief that everything will work out for my benefit, and I will emerge as the victor. To quote Epictetus: "It's not what happens to you, but how you react to it that matters." While I cannot control everything in life, I possess the power to choose my response to the unknown. I am growing stronger because I am choosing to think differently. Finding the good in this situation is challenging, but I am doing my best to find meaning and purpose amidst the pain. This experience is teaching me resilience and enabling growth through trauma.

# CHAPTER 3

## Diagnosis Day

"Never give in and never give up."

— HUBERT H. HUMPHREY

Finally, the day arrives for the announcement of the biopsy results, Thursday, July 2nd, 2020. Originally scheduled as a telephone appointment, I received a call asking if we can meet face-to-face. The change in plan hints at bad news. My left breast is still incredibly sore from the biopsy and the anaesthesia.

And then, they deliver the news. It is the dreaded "C" word. The biopsy confirms that I have cancer, a tumour in my left breast. Paralysed and in a state of shock, I struggle to recall much of the conversation.

Thankfully, the nurse is jotting down notes and atten-
tively listening. Everything looks bleak. Disbelief,
shock, and confusion flood my mind. The cancer diagnosis leaves me feeling weak and helpless. The consultant explains that I require an urgent operation to
remove the tumour. They do their best to reassure me,
sharing that it is a Grade 1 cancer (there are four grades
of cancer), that it is oestrogen receptor positive, and
that chemotherapy is unlikely to be necessary.

The plan is to remove the cancerous tissue from the
breast and, simultaneously, remove the lymph nodes
under my armpit to ensure there is no evidence of the
cancer spreading. Following the operation, I will
undergo radiotherapy and take an anti-estrogen tablet.
**However, the consultant cautions that things may
change after the operation when the full results
are available – and that is precisely what happens.**

My surgery is scheduled for two weeks from today, on
July 15th, 2020. The consultant mentions that I will
undergo a lumpectomy. The truly daunting aspect is
not knowing whether the cancer has spread or how
aggressive it is. I won't have this information until the
operation, when the lymph nodes are removed and
sent for testing. The waiting period proves to be the
most challenging part. I refuse to let this situation

define my self-perception. I refuse to let it intimidate me. I begin preparing by reading scriptures, listening to comforting music, and praying. These practices fill me with hope, encouragement, and peace. Hebrews 11:1 resonates within me: "evidence of things not seen." Faith surpasses feelings, sight, taste, and hearing, affirming their reality. This becomes my key to experiencing the miraculous and what sustains and protects me in this situation. I emerge with a sense of victory, free from panic. Additionally, as an Australian, I adopt the great Aussie deflection: *"She'll be right, mate."*

I turn to the Bible and discover the gift of hope, bestowed to assist us during times of need. Hope is a shield and weapon against problems. The Bible teaches that hope is a virtue, instilling courage and confidence that things will ultimately turn around for the better. I refuse to host a pity party; instead, I surrender myself to my heavenly Father and the entire medical process as it unfolds. I know I am in one of the best hospitals with countless supporters. I maintain hope that I am in good hands and focus on what truly matters, making the best of the situation.

I made the decisive decision to get up and go out for a walk with my family as I find this very relaxing. I refuse to wallow in self-pity. From a young age, I have always cherished the outdoors, perhaps due to being born in Australia, where the weather is often hot and glorious, and nature beckons. It's a lovely weekend, and I relish walking both in the countryside and along the coast. I immerse myself in the scenery, appreciating the beauty and serenity of nature. These walks provide me with an opportunity to pray, evoke positive emotions, and offer moments of restoration and new insights.

After our family walk, I sit down with the children to explain that mummy has a lump in her breast. I reassure them that I will go to the hospital, where they will remove the bad lump and put me back together, making everything well again. I also mention that during this time, I may not feel well due to hospital visits. I constantly reassure them that I will not die. They read a book given to me by the nurse and ask numerous questions, including whether I will lose my hair.

Initially, I find it challenging to process the news, and my mind works overtime. However, I try not to over-analyze the results and instead go with the flow, trusting the tide that carries me forward.

During this prolonged and arduous waiting period, I must learn to trust in God and His involvement throughout the entire process. I turn to Psalm 54, which speaks of finding strength during crises. I cry out to God, expressing my honest emotions. I confess that I don't understand why this is happening, but I implore His help to navigate through it. My church leaders pray with me via Zoom as we practise shielding. During this waiting period, my character undergoes refinement. I learned that it's not about waiting for the storm to pass but rather rejoicing in the midst of it. Trusting God and worshipping Him while still in the midst of a crisis requires self-control and courage. It reframes every difficult moment, reminding me of a sermon I once heard in Australia, which proclaimed that God assigns the toughest journeys to the strongest soldiers because they are the ones capable of enduring. I remind myself that I can handle this battle because God has provided me with His strength and the tools to overcome.

Patience is the ability to accept or tolerate delay without becoming anxious or annoyed. It is the exercise of sustained endurance. In other words, patience is not just about waiting; it's also about how we behave during that waiting period as we strive for the desired outcome. This is where I find myself now. I recall the nine months of patience endured during my four pregnancies to bring forth the fruits of labour. It required immense patience. Now, my patience is expanding as I reflect upon how fortunate I am that the lump was discovered, that I am alive, and that God will grant me the grace to navigate this situation. The road ahead may be painful, but if I endure, I will reap the rewards. I must persist, be patient, and emerge from this season healthier and stronger.

"Heavy is the crown and yet she wears it as if it were a feather, there is strength in her heart, determination in her eyes and the will to survive resides within her soul. She is you, a warrior, a champion, a fighter, a queen."

— R.H. SIN

CHAPTER 4

## The Operation

"You can often change your circumstances by changing your attitude."

— ELEANOR ROOSEVELT

The day of the operation had arrived. Unfortunately, due to the lockdown, I had to go alone. No one was allowed to accompany me. I reminded myself that even though I felt alone, my Creator God was with me, providing comfort. I woke up extra early and spent time with my creator and what stood out from this time was that even in the midst of our problems, we can still hold onto our joy. I focused on the fact that God sees the bigger picture, knows everything, and is actively working in the situation. I recognised that although I may not currently have strength, it will come, which fills me with hope.

We were going to pull and rip this cancer out of my body completely. I desperately wanted this thing gone, never to return. None of us want to die; we all have so much to accomplish and big plans for our lives. The nurse and consultant visited me, engaging in everyday conversations to put me at ease while marking my body around my nipple, armpit, and the side they would use to reconstruct my breast.

I then had to wait for what felt like an eternity to be called into the operating theatre. It wasn't until late afternoon, about six hours after my arrival, that my name was finally called. They were ready. I was wheeled into the operating room, where I was greeted by my good friend, Mr. Arul Immanuel, a Consultant Oesophago-Gastric Surgeon, who was working that day. He held my hand and prayed for me with a compassionate and caring look in his eyes. His soothing and comforting prayer meant a lot to me.

This was an important moment of support during this challenging time and brought me much happiness. I was also introduced to the friendly anaesthetist, who held my hand to calm my nerves. The needle entered my hand, and then I drifted off to sleep.

The operation went well, but due to COVID-19 restrictions, I had no one waiting for me as I emerged from the theatre and returned to my bed. I would have loved to have been welcomed by visitors, which would have made me feel better, but I was grateful that God was by my side and that I was alive. I experienced soreness, and I couldn't move or lift my arm beyond halfway. Lifting, even something as simple as a kettle, was not possible. I had to rest and put my feet up.

In the weeks following the surgery, my arm remained heavy and stiff. I couldn't lift it beyond eye level. I had to keep doing exercises given to me by the nurse so that my arm movement would not be restricted. The most important thing was that the cancer had been removed from my body. I refused to let cancer gain the upper hand. The nurse also informed me about lymphedema, a potential swelling or fluid collection that I could experience for life due to the removal of my lymph nodes.

I have been overwhelmed by the love and support I have received. Friends have shown intentional and genuine care for me, and it has been like heaven. I received food deliveries, flowers, texts, phone calls, and gifts. People have gone the extra mile with their kindness, generosity, and time. Nigerian food kept arriving at my door, prepared with love by my Nigerian sisters – delicious rice, chicken, beef, and stew. I absolutely adore Nigerian cuisine, with its freshness, colours, flavours, and spices. I cherished these delightful moments.

People helped with school runs, childcare on weekends and holidays, and shopping. I felt immensely blessed to have such a caring and loving network in my church, among friends, and within the community. I knew I was not alone; together, we would navigate through this. I am eternally grateful for this support. These triumphant moments, sometimes found in the smallest gestures, fortified my faith.

CHAPTER 5

## When Life Sucks

"Sometimes life will kick you around, but sooner or later, you realise you're not just a survivor. You're a warrior, and you're stronger than anything life throws your way."

— BROOKE DAVIS

The day arrived for me to meet with the breast consultant to discuss the biopsy results. It was a serious conversation about gradings and size, and there was a lot of information to take in at the time.

Unfortunately, the operation revealed that my cancer was more serious than initially thought. I had not one, but three cancers in my breast. The largest cancer was a

Grade 3, moving to Grade 4, measuring 45mm, and there were also cancer deposits in my lymph nodes. As a result, the treatment plan had to be adjusted, and I now require chemotherapy and radiotherapy. This news was not what I wanted to hear; it changed everything. Previously, they thought I only had Grade 1 cancer and would require radiotherapy. But now, it was between Grade 3 and 4. How did this happen? From a diagnosis of stage 1, I now faced a Grade 3 moving to Grade 4 cancer. Despite this devastating outcome, I had to make up my mind to let go and trust God to carry me through this. In reality, of course, doing this was anything but easy.

Since my breast cancer tested positive for oestrogen receptors, I would be taking a daily hormone therapy tablet called Tamoxifen. This medication would help stop oestrogen from causing any breast cancer cells to grow, and I would need to take it for five or ten years. After finishing chemotherapy, I would also undergo radiotherapy. The chemotherapy cycles would occur every three weeks.

They explained all the potential side effects of chemotherapy, which sounded daunting and scary. I was not excited about the thought of losing my hair, experiencing fatigue, nails falling off, headaches, dry throat and mouth ulcers, aching joints, or having horrible skin and nausea.

However, no matter how terrible it sounded, I refused to let this cancer bring me down. Fear tried to take hold—fear of losing my children, fear of death, and fear of missing out on my aspirations, dreams, and plans. I could choose to be a victim and let my emotions rule my life, or I could face this head-on, one step at a time, and keep telling myself that I could do it.

The diagnosis reminded me of how fragile life is. In order not to let my emotions get the better of me, I had to focus on the facts: how long I could expect the effects to last, the finish dates, and the wonderful things to enjoy in the process. Yes, it was a battle, but I knew the outcome, and I certainly was not going to lose.

The lesson I learned here was to put things into perspective. I thanked God for being alive. I was grateful that I had pain and a lump in the beginning, which led to the discovery of the cancer. I kept my mind focused and maintained a positive attitude. We have the power to choose positivity and gratitude, and it makes a difference. Just breathe and do not give power to the enemy. You are a winner. Choose hope even in difficult seasons, as it requires immense courage. Anxiety can destabilise the mind, but we must stay strong when faced with challenges. From my upbringing, I learned that no situation can overwhelm us. Circumstances may bring us down, but God wants us to carry on, bring renewal, and embrace life. Despite everything my mum went through, she remained thoughtful and strong, a beacon of hope and life. Though I didn't feel optimistic, I clung to hope and sought a better and richer way out of this trauma. I chose to believe, starting small, and in turn, creating more hope. I felt connected to my mum, who lived in hope and chose a happier way of life. I also read inspirational stories to help me move towards that blue sky in the midst of a gloomy day.

CHAPTER 6

## In the Hurricane

"Then we cried out, "Lord, help us! Rescue us!"
And he did! God stilled the storm, calmed the
waves, and he hushed the hurricane winds to only a
whisper. We were so relieved, so glad as he guided
us safely to harbour in a quiet haven."

— PSALM 107:28 (TPT)

With the news of cancer, I feel like I've been thrown into a hurricane without warning. This is not what I signed up for. I cried out to God, pleading for this season of my life to end because it would disrupt everything. I wanted God to miraculously remove this from my life without having to go through the journey, but He had different plans. After a couple of days, I accepted the diagnosis and stopped resisting the treatment. God reassured me that He would journey with me. He silenced the storm, calmed the hurricane in my life, and provided me with peace and the assurance that He was with me. I am not ignoring the diagnosis; instead, I am choosing to rise above it. This experience is increasing my faith and helping me emerge stronger.

Being a child of God became my superpower. It sustained, protected, and strengthened me throughout. The knowledge that I am a royal daughter stayed with me, giving me confidence, peace, and purpose.

To navigate this journey, I had to take one step at a time, even though I wanted everything to be done and removed at once. I had to let go and begin with small steps. There is power in the process of this journey as I get closer to removing cancer from my body. I completed one step—the operation—and now I am about to embark on the next step, chemotherapy. At each step, I offered a heart of gratitude, saying, "Another one bites the dust!" I kept my eyes focused on one step at a time throughout the treatment process. After each round of chemotherapy, I persevered and didn't back down. With every step, I expressed gratitude, knowing that I was getting closer to wiping out and destroying the cancer. Each step may have seemed slow and small, but I never gave up or backed down. I kept my eyes fixed on the end process, knowing that I would reap the fruits of my efforts and achieve victory. All those small, continual steps of the journey added up to an overall successful outcome—a cancer-free, healthy life.

In this difficult stage of the journey, I remain focused and disciplined because there is so much to live for. I believe mountains will be moved, and I will reach the other side—healthy, whole, and cancer-free. These dark and silent seasons in our lives are especially important as they develop strength and other important character traits in our lives so that we can be fruitful and blossom.

If you find yourself in one of those difficult and dark seasons, hang in there and keep pushing forward, one step at a time. Be cautious about how you respond during the season of waiting and silence. I wouldn't be here today if I hadn't persevered through this season. I kept reminding myself that this is just a temporary season I am passing through, and at the end of it, I will emerge with a new body and perspective. Stay focused and make your life a priority.

# CHAPTER 7

# Chemotherapy

"Never give up, for that is just the place and time that the tide will turn."

— HARRIET BEECHER STOWE

M y first chemotherapy session was booked for Friday, 11 September 2020. I had the weekend off before starting chemo to celebrate while I had the chance. It is recommended to get your hair cut short before you start chemo to make the ordeal a little less traumatic. I was willing to sacrifice my glorious hair for the fight. I decided to make this Saturday a time for self-care, which involved getting my haircut and styled, having lunch, and applying makeup. My hairdresser recommended a

graduated bob with layers, and then she curled my hair
for me. It looked fabulous, and it became one of my
last moments before I lost my hair. I reminded myself
that I am worthy of love and that I am going to look
my best. I also made time to go for a walk, one of my
favourite hobbies, to refresh myself for what lay ahead.
In my daydreams, I transformed this dismal, gloomy,
and harsh time into a place of colour, glitter, and glam.
I tapped into the belief that I am alive and winning.
This hope carried me through the moments of pain,
suffering, and grief, creating the conditions for hope to
bloom and inspiring me with cheer.

On my way to the hospital for my very first chemo
session in September 2020, I wasn't allowed to have
anyone accompany me due to the coronavirus. I had to
sit and wait for what felt like ages in the waiting area
for my name to be called while they prepared the
chemo drugs. As I waited, I took a deep breath and
spoke to myself as if I were my mum trying to talk
sense into me. I asked myself, *"Kerrie Ann, what are
you frightened of? You know who you are and to whom
you belong. Just walk in there confidently with your head
held high and embrace the process."*

I waited for an hour, and by the time my name was
called, I was relaxed and confident. As I walked into

the room, I felt the presence of God. It felt like I heard His voice and my mum's. The nurse weighed me, performed the necessary checks, gave me some steroids, inserted the needle, and connected me to tubes and bags. There was a pink/red sac of fluid and a clear fluid sac. The nurse explained that my urine would turn a pink/red colour. One bag was completed, and it was time for the next one. It took a while as the liquid flowed slowly. The entire process took close to three hours.

I was informed that if my temperature went over or under certain points, I should not hesitate to go to A&E, as chemotherapy lowers the immune system and makes me vulnerable to infection. With young children and in the middle of a pandemic, I refused to be daunted by these frightening and unnerving side effects. It was a challenge, but I wasn't giving up without a fight. I was constantly reminded of the many side effects and risks associated with chemotherapy, and I was well aware of them from seeing what it did to my mother. But I wasn't going to let fear consume me. I reminded myself that God was safely by my side, sheltering and protecting me from the dangerous side effects and complications.

After my very first chemo session, I felt weird, shaky, and dizzy. I felt awful. My legs were shaking, and I swayed as if I were drunk. That night, I experienced sickness, diarrhoea, and a lot of joint pain. Completing just one session made me ponder how I would get through another four months of treatments. I won't lie —chemotherapy is horrific. It drains everything out of you. The treatment is overwhelming and harrowing. In those moments, I had to carefully choose my thoughts and words. Chemotherapy may have been taking a toll on my physical body, but it wasn't taking away my strength and sense of humour. I knew deep down that victory was mine. I kept reminding myself that this was just a chapter of my life; it was not the whole story.

The injections I received for a whole week immediately following each cycle of chemotherapy were horrendous. They were injected into my tummy each day for a week. These injections, called G-CSF injections, boosted my white blood cell count. However, they landed me in A&E. It started with joint pain in my back, legs, and jaw, chest pain, breathlessness, bruising, and nosebleeds. The pain became worse, and my back muscles started to spasm. I was in agony, unable to breathe, walk, or even talk. By 1 am, I was in hell. The spasms were unbearable. I received morphine to alleviate the pain. Every time I had these injections, I experienced excruciating pain in my bones, insomnia, breathlessness, chest pain, loss of balance, headaches, earaches, and my face turned red.

The chemotherapy treatment and injections made me feel as if I was running a marathon. I was exhausted, drained, and in pain. But I was determined not to let this cancer define me or put me in a box. I told myself, 'You've got this, girl.' I refused to let negative attitudes and emotions rule over me. I was determined to come out of this experience with victory. I remembered what a friend once told me—that challenges can become stepping stones to greatness—and it reaffirmed my outlook. I chose hope over fear.

While sitting in the chemotherapy ward of the hospital during my treatment, I met many other people going through their own challenges. I had the opportunity to interact with them, and it humbled me. I learned that even in our darkest seasons of life, such as the trial and challenge of cancer, we can reach out to those around us and make a positive impact in their lives. Despite our own struggles, we can still bloom and flourish. As Mother Teresa said,

"Be happy in the moment. That is enough."

CHAPTER 8

*Hair Loss*

"Do what you can, with what you have, where you are."

— THEODORE ROOSEVELT

I t was shortly after my first chemotherapy session that my hair loss began. It happened suddenly, with great big clumps of hair falling off my head and covering the kitchen floor. I was told that I wouldn't lose my hair until after a few chemotherapy sessions, but it all fell out within two weeks of my very first chemo. This indicated that the chemotherapy was powerful and working in my body. Unable to bear the hair loss any longer, I went to a local salon and had it all shaved off. I left the salon wearing a beanie, wondering what my children would say when they saw my bald head. I looked completely different. Thankfully, I got a wig fitting before all my chemotherapy started as I envisaged that I might not feel well enough later on. I'm grateful that I did—it was the free one provided by the NHS. Since we were still in lockdown, I didn't go out in public anywhere except for hospital visits.

I had two synthetic wigs. I certainly was not going to pay a fortune for human hair, and the idea of wearing someone else's hair on my head felt weird to me anyway. I didn't wear the wig all the time, as it made me hot and uncomfortable, and I worried about it slipping or blowing away. Instead, I often chose to embrace my bald head and wore scarves or beanies.

Losing my hair was distressing and initially painful, and I constantly felt the cold on my head without any hair. However, as I stood in front of the mirror in my bedroom, looking at my bald head, I began to see my new look with a fresh perspective. Rather than being upset by my appearance and the pain, I focused on my blessings—being alive, having the ability to see, and receiving treatment in a great hospital. The blessings were endless. This bald head was just a small part of the challenges people are facing around the world. I grew accustomed to my bald head and told myself that I am still an amazing and beautiful woman. I am still Kerrie Ann. I found contentment and felt blessed. I had sacrificed my glorious hair to fight this battle, and I was determined to cross over to the other side, knowing it was worth the fight.

# CHAPTER 9

# Great Things Happen When People Pray

"Tremendous power is released through the passionate, heartfelt prayer of a godly believer."

— JAMES 5:16 TPT

"It is only in sorrow that bad weather masters us; in joy we face the storm and defy it."

— AMELIA BARR

Since starting this treatment, I've developed a dislike for having my blood drawn. I need to have my blood tested a day or two before each chemotherapy session to determine if the treatment can proceed. My veins have become swollen and damaged from months of injections. The nurses struggle and swear as they try to find a usable vein. Every time the big needle comes out, I look away. It takes multiple attempts in various spots just to get a vein. Bruises are left behind as a battle ensues to extract the blood.

The first round of chemotherapy hit my body hard due to my compromised liver function. My liver enzyme levels remained elevated at 200, when they should be below 64. This means that my second cycle of chemotherapy will be delayed until my liver function improves. The chemotherapy makes me feel sick, exhausted, and nauseous. Even climbing the stairs in my house becomes a challenge, as I have to hold onto the rail, take breaks, and sometimes crawl up step by step. The chemotherapy has caused my face to swell and become red. I've also lost my eyelashes and most of my eyebrows. My entire body feels puffy, heavy, and swollen with fluid.

I often wonder how long this will go on. I long to be done with this process and come out on the other side. But I must not rush the process, for it is in this journey that great and wonderful things are emerging. I reflect on the qualities that are being developed through this challenging season: endurance, peace, joy, perseverance, patience, and love. God is bringing out greatness through this hardship. I must be intentional and serious about navigating through it. Yes, chemotherapy has shaken me to my core, but I've chosen to shift my focus to my blessings. I must stay the course, knowing that I'm headed towards a cancer-free future. I welcome this challenge, stepping out of my comfort zone and into the unknown. I am determined not to retreat. I'm grateful for the amazing people who surround me, lifting my spirits. I am fully aware that God is on my side, uplifting my mood.

I'm thankful that many people have been interceding passionately for my health. I feel the calmness, security, and safety that comes from knowing people are praying for me. Their prayers carry supernatural strength. In the face of adversity, the prayers, messages, texts, and surprises mean a lot to me. They encourage me and help develop resilience. These are extraordinary moments within the ordinary, glimpses of heaven on earth.

The second cycle of chemotherapy had to be delayed by two weeks due to my liver function. Finally, my blood levels dropped down to 64, allowing me to proceed with the treatment. This delay turned out to be a blessing in disguise, as it gave my body much-needed rest and rejuvenation. I didn't beat myself up over the delay. Instead, I used it as an opportunity to reflect and regain strength for the journey ahead.

Incontinence has become an issue due to the effects of chemotherapy. My body is in a frail state, causing my bladder to malfunction. I now wear large pads to manage it. Despite not feeling great, I choose to stay grateful for being alive and maintain connection with my friends and family. This brings a sense of happiness. A positive attitude directly impacts wellbeing and recovery.

Life presents challenges that can try to pull us under. At times, they may feel insurmountable. We must rise above them by focusing on the positive and acknowledging the progress we've made. Remember, there is always an end to the challenges and seasons we find ourselves in.

During this process, I've learned the importance of slowing down. I used to race through life, going from one thing to the next. It took a major illness to change that mindset. I remind myself that tomorrow is a new day and to conserve my energy. Life isn't always fair. If this storm hadn't happened, perhaps I wouldn't appreciate the beautiful days to come. I remain hopeful.

Though I may not have strength at the moment, it will come. Better days are on the horizon.

I am a Proverbs 31 woman who arms herself with strength. I choose to embrace that strength. We all have weaknesses, but I refuse to use them as an excuse to give up. I won't merely make it through the day; I will journey forward with hope and a renewed passion for life. When I look in the mirror at my bald head, I remind myself that I am a work in progress. God created me wonderfully as a human being. I am comfortable in my own skin, even without hair, eyebrows, and eyelashes. This diagnosis has been a blessing, for it has changed my perspective and refocused my energy on what truly matters in life.

# CHAPTER 10

## She is Strong

"She is clothed with strength and dignity; she can laugh at the days to come."

— PROVERBS 31:25 NIV

The second cycle of chemotherapy was horrendous. The joint pain, nausea, dizziness, incontinence, aching, and fatigue were unbearable. Remembering it all also reminds me how much I hated chemotherapy; it made me feel sick. I could not sleep at night as I was in so much pain, and the morphine prescribed for pain relief only adds to the nausea and dizziness. I spend most of my time on the sofa, dozing off while sitting upright to avoid the feeling of the room spinning when I lie down.

Despite feeling poorly due to the side effects, I am grateful for the cooked meals provided by my friends for my family. Cooking was once my hobby, but now I rely on others to help. This shift from independence to reliance on others has been challenging, but given the pain and weakness in my body, I appreciate the assistance and care. Cancer cannot diminish who I am on the inside. I remain strong, enthusiastic, and determined.

The following verse from a bookmark, which was given to me by my aunty at my mum's funeral reminded me about what cancer cannot do in one's life.

## WHAT CANCER CANNOT DO

It cannot cripple love
It cannot shatter hope
It cannot destroy peace
It cannot kill friendships
It cannot suppress memories
It cannot silence courage
It cannot invade the soul
It cannot steal eternal life
It cannot conquer the spirit

The days feel long and difficult. Cold winds howl outside on this November afternoon. I remind myself to take one day at a time. I am the master of my destiny, the one thing I can control. There is a reason and purpose to this journey, and God will be glorified through it. I will not merely get through this process; I will emerge with new aspirations and a zest for life. I will flourish, and this journey will forever shape me. I pause to breathe and reflect, acknowledging my progress. I offer gratitude to God for both the good and the bad experiences.

To help me relax, I recite my favourite scriptures while wrapped in a fleece blanket on the sofa. This practice prevents negative thoughts and fears from taking hold, reminding me that God has not abandoned me and that I am precious in His sight. The words of Apostle Paul to the Philippians encourage me:

> "I find the strength of Christ's explosive power infuses me to conquer every difficulty."
>
> — PHILIPPIANS 4:13 TPT

Though it is tough, I maintain a positive outlook. I am not alone in this battle. I affirm, "I can and will defeat this. I will emerge victorious." This period of treatment allows me to reassess my life and envision the life I desire. Once treatment is complete, I will prioritise my health and live that life fully. I will not rush but take good care of myself to be present for my family. Sleep will be a priority. I am determined to embrace life to the fullest. The promises of hope in the Bible expand my soul and mind, and I am surprised by the good things God brings into my life. My imagination is captivated by the possibilities.

Though impatience tempts me to rush through treatment, I understand that I must go through each stage to reap the rewards of a cancer-free body. I stay on course, knowing that this journey is changing my life for the better. I remind myself that I am moving in the right direction, sustained by God's grace.

To help me endure each stage of chemotherapy, I celebrate with a small reward after each round. I look forward to indulging in activities I love, such as watching a movie, enjoying scented candles, savouring chocolate, spending time with my children, and reading. These little treats serve as incentives, reminding me that I am one step closer to my goal. Each small step contributes to the bigger picture of a healthy, cancer-free body.

These moments of pleasure in the midst of my darkest days provide a glimmer of hope for tomorrow. They offer respite from suffering, even if just for a short while. My mother taught me that what goes down must come back up, and I hold onto that belief. I will bounce back from this trauma and overcome these challenges with faith and resilience. I am unstoppable.

# CHAPTER 11

# Self-Care, Indulgence and Happy Memories

"The most important relationship in life is the one you have with yourself."

— DIANE VON FURSTENBERG

"Sit. Feast on your life"

— DEREK WALCOTT

I n December 2020, I entered menopause at the age of 44 as a result of the treatment. Steroids and treatment have caused me to gain weight, and I now experience hot flushes. My eating habits have changed drastically since the start of treatment. Nausea and indigestion lead me to snack on sweet things, particularly chocolate. My taste buds have completely shifted. I constantly have a sore mouth, as if it's filled with metal. Chemotherapy also causes sores on my tongue and throat, as well as irritating mucus. All I crave are small sugar snacks that bring me temporary relief from nausea. Indulging in these treats makes me feel better and allows me to momentarily escape the harsh effects of chemotherapy. The deliciousness of these snacks brings me joy with every scrumptious bite.

Before chemotherapy, I prioritised exercise and healthy eating. My current eating habits are unlike me. I consume chocolate every day, and the thought of salads and vegetables makes me nauseous. I'm not sure if it's the drugs in the chemotherapy or if I'm turning to comfort food to alleviate nausea, or perhaps it's a combination of both. Regardless, I hold onto the vision that once treatment is over, I will return to healthy eating and take care of my body, my temple.

I remind myself not to put too much pressure on me during this temporary phase of my life. It's important to make time to enjoy myself. Life is short, and allowing oneself moments of enjoyment leads to improved well-being. I've learned that surviving challenging times requires taking care of oneself and getting the rest my body needs.

This experience has taught me the hard way the importance of dedicating time to myself. As a working mother of four children, I often placed myself at the bottom of the list, caught up in the never-ending tasks of homework, cooking, washing, lessons, cleaning, bills, and sports. Neglecting my own needs led to burnout and exhaustion, which are detrimental to both my health and my ability to care for my children. Although it initially felt selfish, I realised that taking time for myself made me a better person, providing me with renewed strength, health, and inspiration. Slowing down, resting, and caring for myself are necessary for enduring this challenging cancer journey. I rely on a higher power, God, to see me through this difficult time and empower me to face each round of treatment.

Finding quiet time away from the chaos and noise of life has been immensely helpful. Stepping away from my children and embracing stillness, peace, and quiet allows me to recharge. I call it my dream escape. I also find solace in keeping a journal and reading. There is always a way forward, and there is always hope.

I recognise my own value and significance, and I am committed to cherishing and caring for myself. Nurturing my physical, mental, and spiritual well-being is essential for remaining strong and flourishing. I have made the decision to prioritise self-care and be purposeful about it to feel my best. Rest and recovery are vital during this phase of my life. I remind myself to be kind and make time for myself. I am creating a life that is unbreakable and filled with joy. I am determined to be happy, regardless of cancer.

God is present in the process, right here with me amidst the mess. My life now revolves around rest, sleep, and eating what I can. I tune out negativity and resist the urge to figure everything out in my mind. I embrace this season of rest, knowing that God is for me and will never abandon me. This carefree attitude is relieving and reduces stress.

Taking the time to get fresh air and engage in uplifting activities is wonderful. Even in a wheelchair, I ventured outside to feel the wind and winter sun on my face. These moments energise me and allow me to focus on my blessings. People from all over have shown me kindness, and I am grateful. Being outdoors gets my blood flowing and offers a reprieve, helping me refocus. These positive habits contribute to a healthier, more fulfilling life for me and my family.

Remember, the appointments and treatments won't last forever. After completing treatment, I will bounce back and emerge as a new version of myself. During this journey, I remind myself to hold on. There is light at the end of the tunnel. Cancer will not defeat me. Instead of succumbing to defeat, I clothe myself with strength to fight for my health. I keep my head up and continue walking through this journey, getting closer and closer to the end. This cancer journey will pass, and I will emerge as a better person. I reflect on the lessons this journey can teach me. As we used to sing in church, troubles don't last constantly. I understand that this is a testing time that will eventually come to an end.

I underwent my operation, chemotherapy, and radiotherapy during a pandemic, which meant I had to shield and couldn't have home visits or receive support from others at my appointments. However, the acts of kindness people extended to me during treatment touched my heart. They shopped for me and brought me cooked meals. Regular prayers over the phone provided me with peace, strength, and comfort. People from all over were praying for me, reminding me that I was not alone in this battle. The grace and love from my church family and friends upheld and sustained me, creating a special bridge of support.

# CHAPTER 12

## I Will

"Patience, persistence and perspiration make an unbeatable combination for success."

— NAPOLEON HILL

Unfortunately, my most recent chemotherapy treatment took a toll on my body. I ended up bedridden for nine days, experiencing severe arthralgia and fatigue. Diarrhoea led to bed sores, and I developed a severely infected paronychia on my big toe. Despite being on my second course of antibiotics, the infection persists, with pus oozing continuously. I feel feverish and endure considerable pain. If the infection doesn't clear, my upcoming cycle of chemotherapy will be postponed, and I won't receive a full dosage due to the impact on my body.

I spend my days lounging on the sofa in the living room, as my body is too weak and helpless to do much else after being on two rounds of antibiotics. Chemotherapy has taken a toll on me—my body is bruised, exhausted, and overwhelmed. I'm even too tired to speak. This experience humbles me and reminds me to be grateful for what I have. Life is fragile and fleeting, but I refuse to be discouraged or give up. I believe there are countless opportunities awaiting me.

During the darkest seasons, it's easy to think that the challenges are insurmountable or that we'll never overcome them. This is when positive thinking becomes crucial. It's difficult to change our thinking and outlook when suffering, but it's essential to focus on good things and speak positive and affirming words. Even when it feels like we're going nowhere, we mustn't give up. I am cultivating positive habits in every aspect of my life—spiritually, physically, emotionally, intellectually, and socially—so that I can thrive, be fruitful, and live a gratifying life with gratitude.

Amidst the trauma, I endure and cherish the wisdom it offers. Scars and wounds have taught me that mere survival isn't enough—I want to soar and thrive. Yes, chemotherapy is dreadful and harsh, but I will tap into my inner strength and persevere. I will transform negatives into positives. I will keep smiling and stay strong. I will remain hopeful and respond positively to this situation. I refuse to withdraw, and I believe the outcome will be remarkable. I will approach life with greater zeal and enthusiasm. I will uncover treasures of hope and joy, precious jewels and diamonds. I will keep going because there is so much to live for and countless possibilities. I am cherished and loved. Extraordinary things will emerge from these difficult and trying times. I live my life in the present moment, with intention, and I don't take anything for granted. Hope and joy are my priorities. Though I've faced tough challenges, I remind myself that I'm still here, adding value to this world. Cancer was a jolt that attempted to shake me to the core, but I inject hope and joy into my life.

As Maya Angelou once said,

> "Each of us has the right, the possibility, to invent ourselves daily. If a person does not invent herself, she will be invented. Be bodacious enough to invent yourself."

# CHAPTER 13

# Christmas 2020

"Christmas will always be as long as we stand heart to heart and hand in hand."

— DR. SEUSS

This year, the children took charge of putting up the Christmas tree and decorating it while we listened to festive songs on the television. The living room was filled with the delightful scent of gingerbread candles, creating a true Christmas ambiance. The kids worked together brilliantly, unpacking all the boxes of decorations. For this year's theme, they chose gold and silver with a touch of red. We also added some delicate glass ornaments, including teddy bears and sparkly baubles. Despite my need to rest and inability to cook, we were blessed with a large turkey, a Christmas hamper, vegetables, chocolates, and thoughtful gifts. The gestures of kindness and support during this festive time touched my heart and left me feeling humbled. Being alive and breathing, I believe it's essential to maintain a grateful attitude, giving thanks for the present moment. Gratitude not only helps us keep things in perspective but also releases feel-good endorphins that we all need.

On Christmas Eve, I underwent my chemotherapy treatment, which meant I could be with my family on Christmas day. Swallowing was difficult, and lumps covered my tongue and throat, leaving me dizzy and unwell. Despite the challenges, I was grateful that the chemotherapy proceeded as planned, albeit at a reduced dosage due to previous infections. I thanked God that I would regain my vibrancy and energy once I passed through this season of chemotherapy. Despite feeling terrible, unable to do much more than lie on the floor due to the pain in my head and eyes, I found moments that were bearable. I affirmed my resilience and embraced the belief that this was my time to shine. After all, it was Christmas—a season of joy and sparkle.

Usually, our family celebrates New Year's Eve at church, but due to the pandemic, we gathered on Zoom. Exhausted and feeling unwell, I made resolutions to not just survive but thrive in this season with God's help. I looked forward to becoming a different person and embracing the future with excitement.

With just one more round of chemotherapy to go, I am incredibly close to completing the treatment. I remind myself that I am moving in the right direction, inching closer to full health.

Sleep deprivation plagues me as the chemotherapy disrupts my ability to sleep. The steroids keep me awake, and dizziness and pain make it difficult to find comfort. However, I remain determined not to let this hinder my enjoyment of life. I consciously choose to focus on thoughts that inspire hope. For example, I think about my four beautiful children. Besides, despite feeling unwell in my body, I know that peace resides in my spirit, and I trust that God will restore me to full health and wholeness. This diagnosis did not catch Him by surprise. He knows my situation and what He is doing.

Finally, the last session of chemotherapy arrives. I am buzzing inside, even though I feel physically exhausted and drained. The cumulative effects of chemotherapy hit me hard—I can barely move, suffer from pounding migraines, and feel constant nausea. I am wobbly, and everything in the room spins. I remind myself that this was the final chemotherapy session. I keep moving forward, even though I feel dreadful. God is still on the throne, greater than my circumstances. Chemotherapy will not rob me of my joy and peace. I declare that my body will recover, and I am strong, victorious, and confident. Finished! I celebrate with applause and a sense of relief. This marks a new day, and the next step on the agenda is radiotherapy, which will commence in a few weeks. Cancer cannot hinder my destiny. Hope stirs within me, and I believe I am making progress, having overcome one significant hurdle.

Throughout this challenging period, it was due to God, my family, and my friends that I was able to shine, persevere, and rise above. I found peace, knowing that God was in control and securely holding me. I encourage you not to give up, as you will rise out of this experience as a stronger person.

I forged ahead through chemotherapy with sheer determination, determined to come out of it with a smile. Each cycle presented delays due to side effects, infections, and abnormal blood work that I had to overcome. There were times when my emotions and the side effects overwhelmed me, leading to despondency and tears. However, I pushed through, refusing to let frustration veer me off track. It wouldn't have helped; it would only make matters worse. Instead, I remind myself not to be too hard on myself when things don't go as smoothly as I hope. I focus on doing my best, expressing gratitude to God and my friends for their support. I am still here, alive, and that is something to be grateful for. I am loved, and people care about me. This experience has left scars, both physical and emotional, but they serve as reminders that I am a survivor.

# CHAPTER 14
## I Will Rise on Eagle's Wings

"Today I will rise.. without doubt or hesitation. Today I will rise without excuses."

— ALEXANDRA FELDNER

"All that is harsh and dissonant in my life melts in one sweet harmony and my adoration spreads wings like a glad bird on its flight across the sea."

— GITANJALI

Feeling the weight of pain and exhaustion in my body, I decided to give myself a much-needed break in a quiet room, accompanied by my favourite music. I played *Eagles Wings* by

Hillsong United—a song that uplifts and brings me comfort. I have come to realise that setting aside time to rest and unwind is not only crucial for my health and well-being but also for my overall productivity and effectiveness. These moments of quiet help me navigate through the difficult days, making them seem less daunting. While listening to the song, I came across a quote by Hafiz:

> "I am a hole in a flute that Christ's breath moves through—listen to the music."

This time of worship feels surreal, and I am filled with the joy of the moment. I let go of anything weighing me down, allowing my spirit to tap into God's inherent strength.

In this rejuvenated state, I feel empowered like an eagle, unafraid of danger. Like the eagle, I am using this stormy time to soar to unimaginable heights of faith. I express gratitude to God for what He has placed in my heart. With His presence, I am fearless and capable of rising above challenges on the wings of an eagle. Indeed", I could relate to the imagery of God Himself as an eagle, as described in Deuteronomy 32,

"He found him in a desert land, and in the howling waste of the wilderness; he encircled him, he cared for him, he kept him as the apple of his eye. **Like an eagle** that stirs up its nest, that flutters over its young, spreading out its wings, catching them, bearing them on its pinions, the LORD alone guided him, no foreign god was with him."

— DEUTERONOMY 32:10–12 ESV

Just as a caring parent eagle attends to every need, the Lord of hosts lovingly watches over his people, safeguarding us (Isaiah 31:5), supplying all our needs (Philippians 4:19), and faithfully remaining with us, never abandoning or forsaking us (Deuteronomy 31:6). This was my experience and testimony. As such, *On Eagle's Wings* became the theme of my journey.

The eagle is unburdened by the cares of the world and the opinions of others. To soar like eagles, we must let go of fear, dread, and any vices that hinder us. If we desire to emerge stronger, we must go through a process similar to the eagle's moulting. During this time, the eagle sheds all its feathers and loses its beak—almost losing everything. It may appear as if it is dying, at its weakest point, but a day comes when the eagle begins to grow new feathers and a new beak, renewing its strength. In the face of weariness, we must hold on, speak positive words to our own souls, and tenaciously embrace hope. Throughout this journey, hope remained my anchor. Despite the many terrible days, I stayed hopeful, opening my soul and spirit to the possibilities of God working everything out.

Walking through this storm has pushed me out of my comfort zone. Due to the pandemic, I spend a significant amount of time alone, allowing me to deeply reflect on myself. I am focusing on areas that need to change, so I can navigate this journey rather than merely drag myself through it. One area that challenges me is self-care. As a mother of four children, I naturally sacrifice and prioritise their needs, often neglecting my own. I feel guilty now, at this stage of life, when I am unable to care for myself. However, I am learning that I need to take time to look after my own needs, not only to give my best to others but also to grow and evolve as a fruitful woman.

I am learning to trust that there is a purpose behind this difficult season. Enduring this thorn, as painful as it may be, I know that I am more than a conqueror. In this journey, I find sustenance, courage, and strength as I feast upon precious promises of hope. I remind myself that this is not my eternal home; I am simply passing through, eventually reaching my destination. Like a flowing stream, I refresh and cleanse myself as I move forward.

Life sometimes delivers powerful blows, but through sheer determination and belief, I know I will make it. I press the reset button, living my life with purpose. I step out of fear and into courage, showing myself compassion. I firmly believe that this experience will not define my entire life, repeating affirmations that I am a wonderful woman who is blossoming.

> "When a storm is coming, all other birds seek shelter. The eagle avoids the storm by flying above it."

> — ANONYMOUS

# CHAPTER 15

# Radiotherapy

"Gratitude is not only the greatest of virtues, but the parent of all the others."

— CICERO

"A woman is like a teabag—you can't tell how strong she is until you put her in hot water."

— ELEANOR ROOSEVELT

To prevent the tumour from returning, I had to undergo radiotherapy. This treatment would begin on 10 February 2021, right in the midst of the frustrating pandemic. I would only have a few weeks break from chemotherapy before starting radiotherapy. I had to go to the hospital every day for the sessions, and because of my age, I had to do a booster session of five additional sessions at the end. The radiotherapy would be scheduled for several weeks.

Before starting the treatment, I had a CT scan so that the radiographers can pinpoint exactly where the radiation will be directed. I have been given a number of tattoos which are like tiny dots and the radiographers precisely draw biro marks all over my chest area to ensure that they target the correct area. The staff tell me I must stay perfectly still and not move so that the rays get to the exact spot. I am still experiencing side-effects from the chemotherapy and when I lie on the treatment table to get zapped the whole room spins as I have dizzy spells which are making me feel nauseous. I am told I am not allowed to move at all from this position to ensure that the radiation only goes to my left breast. I experienced redness, burning pain, swelling blisters, soreness and fatigue as the radiation built up. But this is nothing compared to chemo-therapy.

On the first day of my radiotherapy, I also started a tablet called Tamoxifen which the oncologist said I have to take daily for five or ten years to stop oestrogen from stimulating any breast cancer cells from growing. The oncologist advised me that these tablets will cause my body to go into early menopause, which is okay as I have been blessed with four children and I used to suffer from very heavy periods. I was informed that it will take roughly three months for the body to adjust. The tamoxifen caused a rash, I feel nauseous and experience uncomfortable hot flushes.

The radiotherapy department was very busy with many people undergoing the treatment. Again, you were not allowed to take anybody in with you for support due to the pandemic. As I sat in the waiting area my eyes were drawn to a little child, a girl who only looked about two years old held in the arms of her mother who was undergoing treatment. This family faced the challenge of caring for this little one who was crying with pain and the anxiety of going in for another day of radiotherapy. It was hard for me to watch this trying to imagine what kind of difficulty this was for a young child to go through. I was extremely humbled by this experience.

On the weekend when I don't have radiotherapy I made time to go outdoors, just to sit and take in some fresh air. This helped me to relax. I just sat there and absorbed the moment enjoying the experience as I listened to the sounds of nature, but I don't sit too long as the wind was always blowing wildly in my face with a chilly feel. I just love the surroundings, and for me, the peace with no distractions helps me crystallise my thoughts.

My last day of radiotherapy was incredibly emotional for me. I got to ring the special bell in the waiting area that signifies treatment has finished with great delight and relief. I would celebrate when I got home with an enjoyable meal and chocolate. After what I have been through, my whole perspective has changed. Material things do not satisfy in the way they did before. I remind myself that I am still here. I am breathing. I am standing. At this moment, I am now stepping onto higher ground. The moment of ringing that bell in the hospital was powerful. I relished the moment. It's a miracle. I was able to ring that bell and slowly walk out of the hospital.

I walked out of the hospital hopeful. This is a journey, and while I have made inroads, there was still a long way to go, but I felt empowered as I was held in the arms of my loving God and supportive friends. That is powerful and it strengthens my spirit.

# CHAPTER 16

## Better Days

"Better is the end of a thing than the beginning."

— ECCLESIASTES 7:8

"You are the storyteller of your own life and you can create your own legend or not."

— ISABEL ALLENDE

After completing five months of chemotherapy followed by radiotherapy, I am now experiencing nightly dizzy spells when I lie down. I struggle to sleep as the room spins, and I wake up each morning with a headache and nausea.

Additionally, my abdomen, legs, and ankles are swollen. This has been going on for several weeks. Despite these challenges, I continue to declare that things will end better and that I will step into better days. It doesn't matter how I started this journey; what matters is how it will conclude. Though my body is weak, my heart remains strong. I understand that my body is still in the process of recovery, and it will take a few more months for the symptoms to disappear. I eagerly look forward to the abundant and fulfilling life that awaits me after all this treatment; that is my vision.

I am grateful to God for the entire experience. Pain teaches you to rearrange your priorities and schedules. Due to this challenge, my life will never be the same. I am thankful that God carried me through this journey, bearing the full weight of the burden so that I did not crumble under its pressure. I am grateful for my friends and family who supported and uplifted me.

I learned not to resist the process but to walk through this journey, allowing it to fulfil its purpose in my life. It was a walk of faith, trusting that God knew all the answers and the final outcome, and that His plans for me were good and perfect. Even though I didn't have all the answers and I experienced pain, I continued to cling to God in faith, knowing that He was my unshakable refuge where I found safety. There is nothing quite like the calm and serene tranquillity that comes from letting go of control and surrendering to God.

This is your life, and you are the storyteller of this incredible journey. Choose to be a legend; choose the path of faith that overcomes and empowers you. If I made it through, so can you. Every step you take is progress. Let your heart and strength shine as you continue to journey forward.

In the midst of the storm, learn to sing, stand calm and still, and smile despite the troubles surrounding you. Trust in God even when the way is rough, stormy, and exceptionally difficult, especially in times of pain. I encourage you to have confidence in the goodness of God, knowing that joy and release will eventually come if you endure this season, one step at a time.

Lesson learned: the antidote to fear is faith.

Something extraordinary happens when you think positively and envision yourself in a way that is not yet revealed. In my mind, I saw myself as whole, healthy, well, and blossoming, and this was reflected in my life.

Your attitude, outlook, and beliefs play a crucial role in shaping your reality and future. I spoke many inspiring and comforting words to boost myself and feel great. I repeated these words and reflected on them daily. It was a choice I made. Finding solace in my own quiet space and speaking affirming words out loud was powerful.

*"I am healthy.*
*I am whole.*
*I am fruitful.*
*I am blossoming.*
*I am worthy.*
*I am strong.*
*I am loved.*
*I am beautiful.*
*I can do all things.*
*I am creative.*
*I am healed.*
*I am making progress."*

Cancer taught me to reframe my mindset. It provided me with a fresh starting point in my life, and I am grateful for this transitional moment. Hope enabled me to keep moving forward, as I had an expectation of a bright future ahead. A wise friend once told me that persevering through pain and distress requires absolute courage, and those words encouraged me. I am on the road to flourishing, bouncing back to a place of healing and restoration.

# CHAPTER 17

## Positivity and Health

"Worry never robs tomorrow of its sorrow. It only saps today of its joy."

— LEO BUSCAGLIA

"It takes a village to raise a child."

— AFRICAN PROVERB

When faced with bad news, such as my diagnosis of cancer, there is no need to despair and lose hope. It is possible to win the battle. I am a living proof of that. However, I made a conscious decision to be positive and grateful. My mindset was focused on defying the odds and living a healthy and fulfilling life. I had numerous reasons to keep living, especially my children. Even in the face of challenges, it is still possible to flourish and succeed by choosing the right words and maintaining a positive attitude. I was determined to live a healthy life and was willing to do whatever it took. Changing my thoughts was the key to bringing about a change in my life. Developing an attitude of gratitude was essential for finding joy in the midst of the dark season I was going through. I had to gather my strength and carry on, embracing the treatment and the process, believing that I would make it. I also had to distance myself from people with negative outlooks in order to protect my emotions and health. Your thinking profoundly affects your health and well-being, so it is important to focus on the good rather than the bad. As King Solomon wrote,

"A cheerful heart is good medicine,"

— PROVERBS 15:30 NIV

and King Solomon wrote,

"Kind words are like honey, sweet to the soul and healthy for the body."

— PROVERBS 16:24 NLT

I learned to make time to smile, even when I didn't feel like it, as it would lift my mood. I was determined not to let cancer affect my outlook on life, which required control, discipline, and purpose. I intentionally focused on things that were encouraging, joyful, and hopeful. I firmly believed that I would make it, that I would be whole and healed. I radiated hope in the face of every obstacle. I practised gratitude daily by focusing on the blessings and good things in life. Surrounding myself with the right people, those who encouraged me and spoke of hope in my situation, was crucial to my journey. I couldn't have succeeded alone, and I am grateful to those special individuals who came alongside me and recharged my life.

Research shows that cancer can be hereditary or develop due to factors associated with an unhealthy lifestyle. In my case, there was a history of breast cancer. Since a young age, I have maintained a healthy lifestyle with proper physical activity and a balanced diet in an effort to prevent such a diagnosis. However, I continue to prioritise my health by eating well, staying fit, managing stress, and getting plenty of rest.

Despite being diagnosed with stage three cancer progressing to stage four, along with all the side effects, and having lost my mother and other family members to this disease, I refused to allow cancer to prevent me from enjoying and thriving in life. When cancer strikes, there is no need to despair and lose sight of who you are; instead, change your attitude. You can be victorious over cancer—I certainly was.

I did not overcome cancer alone. The saying "it takes a village to raise a child" proved true in my journey through cancer treatment. It was a communal effort, with the support of neighbours, friends, family, and church community members all playing a part. I am deeply grateful for their love, support, reassurance, and advice. Our lives, as well as the lives of our children, have been enriched by their presence.

Every day is an opportunity to take a new breath, to live life with joy, gratitude, and fun. The fact that we wake up with our faculties intact and can take each step is a blessing. I am committed to making myself whole by channelling my energy towards compassion, kindness, love, and gratitude. I aim to embrace the present moment, without dwelling too much on the future or lamenting past mistakes.

As a breast cancer survivor, I have discovered the meaning of how I want to live my life—a positive transformation. We all will face death at some point, and confronting this reality can help us live with greater intention and care.

CHAPTER 18

# Who Are You?

"I am large, I contain multitudes."

— WALT WHITMAN

When facing challenges, it is common to lose focus and become dissatisfied and discouraged. In such moments, it is important to refocus on who you are and what you have to offer. I made the decision to align myself with God against my own emotions and feelings when cancer rocked my world. I knew that I was a warrior, a queen, loved, and secure. Winning can become a habit and a lifestyle for anyone.

Protecting your mind and speaking positive and encouraging words over your life are crucial. James in the Bible tells us that our words have immense power and can cause destruction. It is important to seize the situation and speak faith into it with good and intentional words. By focusing on your blessings, your health, and the people around you, you deny cancer any power. The words I spoke into my situation helped me overcome; words like "arise," "take courage," and "thrive." I remained focused and believed that I would make it. Instead of dwelling on what I didn't have, I chose to focus on the many blessings I did have. This change in perspective helped me triumph over cancer. I knew that a day would come when I would no longer struggle with my health and that wholeness was on the horizon. I was determined to blossom once again.

I learned to enjoy, appreciate, and savour each present moment rather than wasting time worrying about the future, which I had no control over. Life is short, and we should look forward to the future with joy. I have tears of gratitude for the love shown to me by my heavenly father and those around me who have unknowingly helped me.

## MY DIARY ENTRY ON NEW YEAR'S EVE 2020

*This year, I was confronted with the shocking news of cancer. Throughout the year, I have seen God carry me and I am blessed to be surrounded by so many loving and caring people. I am blessed not because of favourable circumstances. I do not despise this season of my life.*

*I will rise above these limitations. I will not just survive the treatment, but I will come out of it thriving, richer, and filled with abundant blessings. I thank you for sustaining me this year and preserving my life so that I can use it to help and encourage others. I am looking forward to a new year and a new me.*

That night, I couldn't sleep and my mind wandered back to the times I visited Fiji, Bangkok, Nigeria, and India, where I met beautiful children with many needs. I was overwhelmed by the immense needs, yet despite their lack of material possessions, these children always had big smiles on their faces and were full of hope, aspirations, and dreams. Many of them aspired to become doctors and engineers.

Those adventurous trips forever changed my life, and I was privileged to be able to make a difference in the lives of others. A sacrifice on my part went a long way in the lives of those children, enabling them to have a better life. I participated in a project in Andhra Pradesh, South India, involving children. We provided support to orphans, ensuring their nutrition and hygiene, and raised funds for training centres to educate and empower the children. Every contribution made a difference, enabling us to bring in more sewing machines for the training centres, where girls were taught sewing skills to create clothing. I was incredibly inspired and excited about the opportunity to raise funds and make a positive impact in the lives of these children. Through a charity auction I organised in Newcastle upon Tyne, we raised £4000, which was amazing and life-changing for the village in Andhra Pradesh. Witnessing the local community come together, giving their time, effort, energy, kindness, and donations to make a significant difference to those overseas was a beautiful sight.

Through this cancer journey, I have discovered a new heartbeat. I now have a greater sense of purpose, motivation, and desire to make a difference in the lives of others, both abroad and in our own community. I have something to offer—hope, a smile, financial support, and services. I have taught my own children that despite what we may be going through, we must think of others, as small acts of kindness can make a huge difference.

I express my gratitude out loud three times. I make time to experience delight. I am grateful for the stamina to keep going. I say thank you again because my faith is strong. Thank you, because I am coming out of the storm. Thank you, as a bright rainbow is emerging. I am blessed because, out of this dark and stormy time, a beautiful, bright, and magnificent rainbow emerges. This is what life is about. I am sustained. I am walking through life with greater qualities now.

"If the only prayer you ever say in your entire life is 'Thank you,' it will be enough."

— MEISTER ECKHART

# CHAPTER 19

# My Family

"While we try to teach our children all about life, our children teach us what life is all about."

— ANGELA SCHWIND

When I was diagnosed with breast cancer, my eldest son Lakemfa was 12 years old, Timiebi my second son was 9 years old, Tahlia my eldest daughter was 8, and my youngest daughter Elicia was 7. With the news of cancer, I am now raising my children with a new sense of energy and outlook on life. Their entire lives and routines were interrupted and turned upside down, and their emotions were running high. It was upsetting to hear the painful questions that arose from school and friends, such as, "I am really worried about my mom, is she going to die?" or "Will mom get better soon or will she always be sick?" We sat them down and lovingly explained that for a period of time I wouldn't be well, that I was not going to die, and that I would get better soon. The children had a good support network where they could talk about what was happening and express their feelings.

I have always been a hands-on mom, always present for the children—school runs, homework, activities, cooking, taking them to parks, walks, and engaging in fun activities on the weekends. Now, with my cancer diagnosis, the children couldn't have playdates anymore. I informed the school about the situation and that their homework might not always be completed. Due to the diagnosis, their lives were interrupted, and they couldn't go on trips, visit friends, go to parks, play sports, bake, or do homework like before. I was undergoing treatment, prone to infection, and often exhausted, spending a lot of time in bed. It was a drastic change for them to be indoors all the time. Due to my low immunity, I wasn't supposed to hug them, although I still did it for emotional support. I am extremely grateful for my four beautiful children who always gave me a reason to keep pushing forward with their laughter and warm hugs. They were amazing and adapted so well when they learned about my cancer.

The children were very helpful and took on new caring roles. To show their love, they would make me drinks, help with housework, and cuddle with me. Timi, Tahlia, and Elicia used their creativity to create cards, drawings, and personalised notes for me. The energy-draining treatment made the children mature and grow in many ways. Of course, they were still children and had their moments of noise and arguments, but that's okay. Their lives didn't come to a halt because of my treatment.

My dear friends, you know who you are, showed so much love to the children in practical ways, such as sweets, craft projects, clothes, dolls, and books—things that the children loved. Through these acts of love, the children learned to appreciate others. They used this time to make gifts for important people in their lives. All these gestures contributed to their mental well-being. I will always be grateful for these special friends.

Through it all, I have learned to spend even more time with my family—laughing, talking, enjoying outings, expressing love, and giving hugs. This journey has changed their perspective as well. We have all weathered the storm together and emerged stronger and more resilient. Our lives have been touched and strained, but we are grateful because we now live with more purpose and abundance.

## CHAPTER 20
# My Mum, It's Mothering Sunday

"My mother is so full of joy and life. I am her child and that is better than being the child of anyone else in the world."

— MAYA ANGELOU

It's Mother's Day, and I want to honour my mother, as she will always be one of my greatest heroes. Mum, you are awesome, strong, courageous, beautiful, and limitless. I owe everything I am to my mother; she is extraordinary. I think of my courageous, gorgeous, and heroic mum who shaped my life. She had a cheerful outlook and a bubbly personality. My mum taught me to appreciate even the smallest things in life. We had a very happy and loving family while growing up. I have many joyful memories. My parents were wonderful; they did everything for us and loved us unconditionally. Despite going in and out of the hospital, my mother rarely complained. She exemplified courage, grace, and endurance in the midst of her gruelling battle with cancer. She went through chemotherapy and radiotherapy for breast cancer, and shortly after, she was diagnosed with terminal secondary cancer. Despite all this, she maintained a strong unwavering faith and lived life to the fullest. Her joy was palpable, drawing people to her. As I sat by my mother's bedside, watching her fade away, I gained great wisdom and learned humility. She inspired and encouraged me, seeing things from a higher perspective, as God might see them. Thoughts of my mum fill my mind with bright colours. I am endlessly grateful to you, Mum. My mother's prayers have followed me throughout my life. Mum lived through unimaginable distress yet radiated with life and positivity. She stood tall, laughed, and always had a smile on her face. Her approach to life is one of the reasons I am surviving and thriving after this traumatic experience.

Her death left me devastated. I cried and grieved, but then I remembered how incredibly strong she was, holding on with courage during that difficult and painful time. She desperately clung to life to see her first grandchild, Lakemfa, but unfortunately passed away three weeks before his birth. That realisation brought some consolation. I will rise and face each day for my mum. To help me through the grieving period, I focused on her qualities, the blessings, and the great things she taught us, as well as her prayers, rather than dwelling on a life taken away.

Then came the arrival of my firstborn, Lakemfa. I truly believe that he was sent from God at the right moment to help our family begin living again. His laughter and cries accompanied us everywhere. To this day, he continues to comfort, love, and bless us with his life.

My mum was hardworking and beautiful. Her wardrobe was always full of vibrant and bold colours - hot pink, deep blue, and rich reds. Her beautiful silver hair, spiky yet soft, always stood out, and she loved wearing bright pink lipstick. I always admired how impeccably dressed and glamorous she was. My mother embodied true natural beauty. She loved making clothes for us and taught fashion and sewing skills at college. She also enjoyed baking and cooking. Mum kept the house immaculate and inspired us to excel. But more importantly, she taught us children the true value of life.

The Bible says,

> "A good woman is worth far more than diamonds... When she speaks, she has something worthwhile to say, and she always says it kindly... Her children respect and bless her"

> — PROVERBS 31 MSG

This perfectly describes my mother, who is truly praiseworthy.

You were always laughing, kind, compassionate, beautiful, and strong. I thank you for teaching me the truth and to stand up for what I believe in. Not only did you impact the lives of your children, but you also touched so many lives around you. You are never forgotten and always missed. Your life was not in vain, and so much of my ability to help and love others has to do with you. I will love you forever.

# CHAPTER 21

# New Life

"The winter is past; the rains are over and gone. Flowers appear on the earth; the season of singing has come; the cooling of doves is heard in our land."

— SONG OF SOLOMON 2:11-12 NIV

S pring is in the air, bringing new life and freshness. The flowers in my garden are slowly emerging with colour and enthusiasm. The shrubs and trees are turning green and growing rapidly. Daffodils have emerged, signalling change all around. The graceful flowers in their rich and vibrant colours represent hope. As the flowers and trees blossom, I am reminded of the abundance in my own life. It is thrilling to see the blue sky and hear the sound of birds singing. I sit in quiet reflection while the children play in the garden. My body is letting go of past experiences and making room for new and beautiful things to come. Spring symbolises the spiritual season of growth and the opportunities that lie ahead.

I enjoy sitting in the garden, making the most of today, absorbing the rays of sunshine, and watching the daffodils sway in the breeze. I live this day with intention, savouring the good moments and being grateful for the gift of an extra day. In many ways, this journey has revealed parts of myself that I was unaware of. The treatment was draining, but a new season of life is on the horizon. I am grateful for the friends who supported me and lifted my spirits along the way. My resilience to cancer has helped me stay afloat. I relish every hour as if it were the last, living life with appreciation, laughter, and joy.

I find myself in a new season of life. Yes, the season of joy lies ahead. The news of cancer invaded my world unexpectedly, but through it all, I learned to stand my ground and position myself to keep moving forward and learning from this season. I want to encourage you to endure the dark and difficult seasons, knowing that the sun will rise again for you. The dark season will give way to beautiful wells of overflowing joy. Live in hope and focus on the things that truly matter in life— joy, gratitude, resilience, and connection.

I refused to be weighed down by the circumstances of this cancer journey. I kept in mind that it had a purpose and continued walking. Life has its ups and downs, its good and bad times. I held on to my belief and dreams of stepping into a new season that would be bigger and greater than yesterday. Hold on and dare to believe. Recognise your talents, values, and worth. Treasure this precious life and savour every moment. I am not defeated; I am victorious. My heart overflows with joy, gratitude, and appreciation for life. I am forming good habits to fully appreciate this moment in my life.

# CHAPTER 22

# *Special People*

"Our greatest fulfilment lies in giving ourselves to others".

— HENRI J. M. NOUWEN

I am incredibly grateful for the special people who provided encouragement and wise counsel during my treatment. I want to share about these individuals who gracefully entered our lives and made a difference. They sacrificed for us, and my heart overflows with gratitude for their love, kindness, and care. Their acts helped lighten the burden I carried. My parents always taught me that as you give to others, it will come back to you. This is exactly what happened to me when I needed it most, as I had sown seeds of help and support throughout my lifetime. As a family, we witnessed the love, compassion, and kindness of humanity in action, and we will never forget it. I hope this inspires you to change your perception. As you bless and enrich the lives of others, it will come back to you, and you too will be refreshed and blessed.

Jacqueline Atkinson (Jackie) is a beacon of life, encouragement, and inspiration. Jackie remembers me in her prayers every day. She has so much to offer—wisdom, practical support, prayers, commitment, and drive. Without fail, every single week she would show up and provide the basic necessities I required when I needed them most. She would also bring special treats for the children, such as sweets, colouring materials, and craft projects. Jackie took the time to talk to them, pray for them, and provide practical and special treats.

Olu Aliu, my lovely sister, would surprise me with parcels containing comfortable clothes that were much needed. She also sent me heartfelt messages. Another friend, Beverley Bond (Bev), sent me a makeup set for Christmas that I had always wanted, bringing tears to my eyes. This eye makeup set made me look and feel gorgeous.

Zara St Clair (Zara) was always busy arranging something to make life better for those in the community.

She used her initiative to organise frozen meals for my family without being asked, which was a true blessing. She also arranged lovely Christmas gifts.

The people from my church consistently and sincerely prayed for me every week, believing that God would perform a miracle in my life and help me through the process. Their prayers carried the weight and burden of this battle, and those moments were filled with wonder. I hold deep respect and love for all these people.

My community nurse was amazing, supportive, and reassuring throughout my journey. She went the extra mile to make me feel at ease. The medical and nursing staff of the NHS (National Health Service) are truly magnificent. The teams at both the Freeman and RVI hospitals in Newcastle upon Tyne were outstanding in their work, showing compassion and kindness. All the staff members were friendly and supportive, and their smiles, kindness, and reassurance made an enormous difference. A massive thank you to all the dedicated medical professionals. I am immensely grateful for the brilliant medical team that surrounded me throughout my entire journey. They made me feel comfortable and special. The staff at the radiotherapy department were particularly incredible. They would call my name from the waiting area, chat with me, and usher me into the room with a friendly and talkative demeanour, providing a comforting distraction. Their caring attitude emphasised the importance of gestures like a warm smile and a kind word, as often we don't know what others are going through, and these small things can make a huge difference. The love shown by these kind nurses was truly a blessing. There are always things to be grateful for and reasons to smile.

I celebrate all my sisters across the world who have fought the battle against breast cancer. I have personally met many of you, and I can testify that you are unique, strong, and amazing. My mother passed away from this disease, but her life remains an inspiration, and she has gone on to live a better life.

# CHAPTER 23

# Moving to the End and Heading to Recovery

"Listen.. you can hear the colours flowering in the quiet of your soul."

— LAUREL BURCH

W ell, cancer did not end my life. This journey pushed me outside of my comfort zone and now I am moving forward. The cancer has been removed, and the treatment has finished, although the effects of chemotherapy still linger in my body. My perseverance and determination have paid off, and I have emerged from the gruelling treatment, entering a new season of flourishing. I feel like a desert finally receiving water, with new life emerging. This was just a season in my life, a daunting mountain that I tackled one step at a time. I was inspired and touched by others in loving and positive ways, which helped me reach the other side cancer-free. I look back upon this journey with a smile. The kindness, mercy, and care I received lifted me up, and now I offer it to you as part of this journey. The treatment was actually a gift that enhanced my life, as I emerged as a healthy and stronger person blessed with the gift of life. The purpose of this journey has been fulfilled, allowing my life and the lives of those around me to flourish and rise to new hopes and aspirations.

This journey has changed my life, prompting me to joyfully consider what I have, who I am, where I have come from, what I have learned along the way, and my aspirations and goals for the future.

I bow down and sing a song of worship, expressing my gratitude to God and all the people who have helped me along the way. Cancer has taught me that even in the midst of pain and suffering, I can still smile, be joyful, grateful, and victorious. Happiness should not wait for perfect circumstances. Make the determined choice to be happy in this very moment, as you may not get another chance to enjoy it. I pause and reflect on all the good things this journey has brought into my life. I am overflowing with hope and living life fully, thanks to the choice I made to wake up each day and say thank you for the gift of the present. I am now in a new season, moving on from breast cancer, but I will never be the same. I will always move forward, aiming higher, pushing boundaries, and creating the life I desire.

After going through this journey, the things I once considered important seem meaningless. The dark and desolate season has taught me to live life with compassion for others and deepened my love for life. Every day brings a chance to breathe, to live without regrets. Now, my body needs more rest to ensure complete recovery. Cancer has taught me to be patient and kind to myself, to avoid rushing. I am standing here, looking forward to my hair, eyelashes, and eyebrows growing back. I am not finished with life; there is still much growing to do. Life is a journey, and while I have made progress, there is still a long way to go.

The sun is shining again. Summer is just around the corner, and I eagerly anticipate spending time with my family, engaging in fun-filled activities I dreamed of during treatment—swimming at the beach, enjoying fish and chips, eating ice cream, and sleeping in tents while watching the stars.

Never take a single day for granted. I have emerged from this experience with a greater sense of purpose, passion, and appreciation for life. It's about being grateful, content, and bringing hope to those around you. This near-death experience has taught me invaluable lessons. When reminiscing about life, no one focuses on bank accounts, but rather chooses to step out and live life to the fullest. I begin to bless my life and sing the song "Blessings" which rejuvenates me. The song states, "Count your blessings, name them one by one, count your blessings, see what God has done." Amidst conflict, great or small, do not be discouraged; God is everywhere. Count your blessings; angels will attend and help and comfort you until the end of your journey. From this journey, I have learned about the amazing power of supportive networks and collaboration. Sometimes, all you need is a little help from your friends and from God to succeed. Remember, you have a special treasure chest within you—your very existence is a gift to this world.

## 25 THINGS CANCER TAUGHT ME

1. Be open to possibilities. I have emerged as a wiser and stronger woman.

2. Do not succumb to fear; face it head-on to overcome it.

3. Break down each stage of the journey into smaller pieces, celebrating each milestone. This approach makes it more manageable and less daunting.

4. Foster positivity in your thoughts and inner self. Focus on the people around you and realise that you are just as deserving of encouragement and love as you bestow upon others.

5. Gratitude allows you to navigate through dark times. Even with cancer, there are things to be grateful for, such as having children, the support of friends, and a place to call home.

6. Embrace new experiences, gain insights, and appreciate the importance of kindness and happiness in contributing to a fulfilled life.

7. Trust God in uncertain and challenging times. This crisis tested my faith, and now it stands at a new level.

8. Approach each day with enthusiasm, even when faced with daunting challenges. Recognize that you are special, brilliant, and amazing. Your past challenges affirm that you

have much to offer and add value to the
world.

9. Be kind and caring; put a smile on someone's
   face.

10. Make time for self-care because you are worth
    it. Just be yourself. Take the time to refresh
    and replenish yourself so that you are not
    running on empty and can better help others.

11. Focus on the present rather than dwelling on
    the past.

12. Fresh air works wonders for the soul and
    body. Embrace greenery, freshness, and
    nature to re-energize your spirit.

13. Enjoy the simple pleasures of life and
    remember that you are not just surviving but
    thriving.

14. Maintain hope. Hope will carry you through
    difficult and despairing days, leading to better
    ones.

15. Take a moment to breathe, slow down, and
    take one step at a time. Just keep moving
    forward; you will get there eventually.

16. Laugh and have fun, as life is short.

17. Think and speak positive and affirming
    words. Surround yourself with wise and

positive people. Cancer has reduced my
tolerance for complaining and trivial talk.

18. Fight for your health and stop engaging in
    activities just for the sake of doing them.

19. Do not take family and friends for granted.
    True prosperity lies in sharing and nurturing
    others.

20. Refuse to settle in this dark season and never
    give up. Reframe your dark times as moments
    of transition.

21. Live an inspiring and generous life.

22. Use this season to work on yourself and make
    the most of it.

23. Life has purpose. Although some days may be
    bleak and awful, maintain hope and believe
    that brighter days are on the horizon.
    Purpose is the life raft that keeps you afloat
    while waiting for the next good destination.

24. Be joyful and grateful throughout the
    journey, rather than waiting for it to be over.
    Otherwise, you will miss the purpose and
    lessons along the way.

25. Be thankful for the journey because it has
    transformed my entire life. Cancer made me
    realise that the small things in life are actually

the biggest and best, such as connections,
laughter, family, and nature.

Remind yourself that you are strong, brave, courageous, and fierce. It is your time to shine. Never forget
that you are inspirational and captivating.

# About the Author

Kerrie Ann, originally from Australia, now resides in Newcastle upon Tyne, UK, where she lives with her four children. In 2020, at the age of forty-three, she was diagnosed with aggressive breast cancer, an experience that motivated her to share her journey in *Wings of Courage* Amidst the challenges of the coronavirus pandemic, Kerrie Ann underwent intensive treatment, including surgery, chemotherapy, and radiotherapy, emerging with a renewed sense of fulfilment and inspiration.

# About the Book

In this heartfelt and insightful book, Kerrie Ann takes us on a personal journey through her experience with breast cancer. The book is not only a memoir of facing a life-altering diagnosis but also an exploration of the strength and resilience that can be found within. With honesty and vulnerability, Kerrie Ann shares the intimate moments, observations, and lessons she learned during her battle with breast cancer. Her story resonates with anyone who has faced adversity while juggling multiple roles and responsibilities. The book offers inspiration and support to those facing similar challenges, particularly individuals diagnosed with cancer and those whose lives are impacted by this disease. The book reminds readers that they are not alone in their struggles and that there is light at the end of the tunnel. Whether you are facing a health crisis, supporting a loved one through a difficult time, or seeking inspiration to overcome personal obstacles, *Wings of Courage* will uplift, inspire, and empower you.

Printed in Great Britain
by Amazon

26098308R00090